THE TWO BUILDERS

Written by Margaret Williams
Illustrated by Steve Smallman

CANDLE
BOOKS

Written by Margaret Williams
Illustrated by Steve Smallman
Copyright © 2006 Lion Hudson plc/Tim Dowley and
Peter Wyart trading as Three's Company

Published in 2006 by Candle Books
(a publishing imprint of Lion Hudson plc).

Distributed in the UK by Marston Book Services Ltd,
PO Box 269, Abingdon, Oxon OX14 4YN

Distributed in the USA by Kregel Publications,
Grand Rapids, Michigan 49501

UK   ISBN-13: 978-1-85985-628-4
      ISBN-10: 1-85985-628-4

USA ISBN-13: 978-0-8254-7315-9
      ISBN-10: 0-8254-7315-2

Worldwide co-edition produced by
Lion Hudson plc, Mayfield House
256 Banbury Road
Oxford, OX2 7DH, England
Tel: +44 (0) 1865 302750
Fax: +44 (0) 1865 302757
email: coed@lionhudson.com
www.lionhudson.com

Printed in China

There were once two men who decided to build a house.

The first man found a nice sandy place,
with a stream gurgling past.

"That's great!" he thought.
"I can't wait to sit outside in the sun."

So he started to build on the sand.

He didn't bother to dig foundations –
he was in far too much of a hurry.

He built his house with stones that were lying nearby.

He put on a wooden roof...

and tiles.

It was quickly finished.

The man sat outside his house in the sun.

But his friend had hardly started!

For his friend had searched carefully
for the best place to build.

At last he found some hard rock.
He dug into it.
It was hard work and took a long time.

He cut a trench in the rock.

Then at last he started to build.

Gradually the walls grew higher.

Finally he added neat tiles…

and a chimney.

At last it was finished.

He was glad to sit down.
He was *very* tired!

But almost at once storm clouds gathered.

The rain fell, the wind blew.
And the little stream grew into a great river.

The two men both raced indoors.

In alarm, they watched from their windows.

The rain fell, the lightning flashed, the thunder roared.

And the river rushed past, wider and stronger.

Then CRRRAASH!!!
The first man's house fell flat!
The foolish man who built on sand
was left with – nothing!

Not even his deckchair.

But in spite of the rain,
the second man's house stood firm.

The wise man had built on rock.
His house was safe in the great storm.

Jesus said,
"People who listen to my words and
put them into action are like the wise man
who built his house on rock."

You can read this story in your Bible in Matthew 7:24–27